BONI LONNSBURRY

creation journal

A Magical Place to Design Your Dreams

InnerArt®
Making your inner art magnificent

Inner Art, Inc.

530 Compton Street #D, Broomfield, CO 80020

www.InnerArtInc.com

Editor: Bryna Haynes, TheAuthorRevolution.com

Cover design and Interior layout : Rachel Dunham and Heather McNamara, YourBrandTherapy.com

Ordering Information

Quantity sales. Special discounts are available on quantity purchases by corporations, associations, and others. For details, please contact the publisher at the address above.

ISBN: 978-1-941322-17-8

1. Nonfiction > Self-Help > Personal Growth > Success

2. Nonfiction > Body, Mind & Spirit > New Thought

table of *contents*

table of *contents*

Welcome, *creator!*

This **Creation Journal** was developed to make the process of conscious creation easier and more elegant. It will help you keep track of your intentions, techniques, signs, action steps, and other details about your creation process. By keeping track of each of the steps, you'll find it easier to stay focused and motivated– and, ultimately, be more successful.

The greatest gift you can give yourself, those you love, and the world at large, is to create the most joyous, successful, and fulfilling life possible. When you're filled with love for yourself and your life, it is easy and natural to love others. And as you lift your vibration to the highest resonance possible, you cannot help but be a positive impact on the world.

Wishing you every blessing and success
in creating a life you love.

With great love,

Boni

you are ***divine***
by your very nature,
you are unconditionally loved, and you have been gifted with the ability to create your own reality.

- Boni Lonnsburry

Working with the Sections

Here are some suggestions and resources for how to work with each section of this journal. You can follow the instructions exactly, or make it your own and work with it in the way that speaks to you. Have fun with it. Enjoy the creation process as much as the manifestation itself, and you'll find it easier and easier to make things magically happen in your life.

My *dream*

This is where you write the "big picture" of what you want. Write it on the Dream page as well as in the Table of Contents. Here is an example:

My dream: "To create work I love."

Next, describe the dream in detail. What does this dream look like? Feel like? How will you know when you have it? Here are some examples:

looks like

I'm not sure what this work will be. The dream is to discover it. But I do know a few things about it. I will be working in a physical location that is beautiful and healthy. I will be working with people that I enjoy. I will be working hours that suit me. I will be making good money at this work.

 *feels*like

As this dream manifests, it fills me with feelings of gratitude, joy, excitement, prosperity, fun, creativity, safety, security, happiness, abundance, and success.

I'll know I have it *when*

There will be stages of manifestation as this dream comes to life.

First, I will begin to have some idea as to what I'd like to create for work. I may experiment with different directions but every experiment will provide me with valuable information on what my ideal work contains.

Then I will begin to investigate, plan, and network how to move forward with the idea that most excites me. Gradually I will begin to do this work in the world and adjust as necessary. And over time, I will become proficient and super successful with this work.

NOTE | **Your intuition and Unseen Friends will show you Information about what your "milestones" are. *Trust them ... and yourself!***

How having this dream *will change my life*

It's important to imagine how creating this dream will change your world. Here's an example:

When I have manifested work I love, I will become more confident. I will feel more empowered. I will be living the life of my truer self. Having created this dream, I will trust myself more. I will be enjoying the hell out of every day. I will feel fulfilled in that I'll be doing the work that is in alignment with my destiny.

My *intentions* for this dream

This is where you write your intentions for this particular dream. You can learn more about intentions at **LiveALifeYouLove.com/resources**.

Here are some examples:

- *I intend to discover work that fills me with joy, excitement, passion, love, abundance, prosperity, and happiness.*
- *I intend to be led to the people, information, resources, and institutions that help me to discover, determine, and develop my ideal work at this time.*
- *I intend that every minute I work be filled with fun, creativity, excitement, abundance, prosperity, joy, and positive surprises.*

- *I intend to allow the unfoldment of my work in perfect timing.*
- *I intend that my work grows easily, elegantly and abundantly and is internally and externally rewarding to the greatest extent possible.*
- *I intend to gratefully and gracefully perform my work on this planet in the perfect timing, with joy and fun, and with the highest level of positive impact possible.*

Techniques I completed

Here, list the techniques you do to "flow energy" to your dream. Some examples are below.

- *The One Minute Manifestor*
- *The Jump the Gap Technique*
- *The Morning Mastermind Technique*
- *The Abundance Ritual Technique*
- *Creating an Abundant Self Image*

All of the above techniques are available at:
LiveALifeYouLove.com/resources.

action steps I took

In this section, list the actions you've taken in the world that have brought you one step closer to your dream. Learn more about "taking action" at **LiveALifeYouLove.com/resources**.

Here are some examples of action steps for the example dream:

- *Made a list of ten people who are my professional heroes*
- *Investigated career counselors*
- *Made a list of my skills and talents*
- *Asked ten friends what they think my skills and talents are, and what career they imagine I'd excel in*
- *Gave myself an hour to sit and think (and write) about what I'd do if I were independently wealthy (given everyone needs meaningful work)*
- *Made a list of ten things I'm interested in, fascinated by, and/or passionate about.*
- *Read the course catalog for a highly regarded school I admire*
- *Remembered my dreams as a child—not to go back to but for clues of my passions/interests*
- *Journaled about the life I desire—not just what I do for work but how I want to live my life, who I want to spend time with, how I want to impact the world, and the values that I hold*

Beliefs I *changed*

List the beliefs you discover and change here. To learn how to change a belief, visit **LiveALifeYouLove.com/resources.**

Here are some beliefs that may require changing to create the dream of work you love, and the corresponding positive beliefs:

I don't know what I'm passionate about.

I can discover what I'm passionate about.

I can't make enough money doing what I truly love.

I can make more than enough money doing what I truly love.

It's a dog eat dog world out there.

It's a loving and supportive world out there.

Most entrepreneurs fail; therefore the odds are stacked against me.

Most entrepreneurs don't know how to create their realities; but I do.

Success is difficult.

Success is easy.

In order to have the work I desire I have to give up some things I value.

I can have the work I desire and all that I value—and more!

Work is hard, boring and thankless.

Work is easy, exciting, and rewarding.

signs I received

You should receive a "sign" that your dream is coming true within three days of doing any powerful technique. Learn more about signs at *LiveALifeYouLove.com/resources*.

Here are some examples of signs you might see for the illustrative dream:

- *You meet a friend for drinks and they tell you about their cool new job.*

- *You come across an article on the internet that indicates job satisfaction is improving.*
- *You have a really great day at your current job.*
- *You watched a movie in which the lead character left a lucrative but unfulfilling career of 25 years to follow their passion.*
- *You begin to be inspired by people you come across online who have similar passions/interests as you.*
- *You visit a new dentist and are amazed at how much they love what they do and by how that is reflected in their practice.*

How I stayed *positive + expectant*

It is important to stay positive for as much of the time as you possibly can in order to allow your dream to come true. Learn more on the Resources page at **LiveALifeYouLove.com/resources**.

Here are some ways one might encourage happiness:

- *Write in my Gratitude Journal*
- *Exercise*
- *Work with my negative self (Learn more at **livealifeyoulove.com/neg**)*
- *Narrow my focus (Learn more at **livealifeyoulove.com/real**)*
- *Take a walk in nature*
- *Set an intention to be happy*
- *Ask my unseen friends to help me stay in joy*

my request for assistance

Write out your request to your Unseen Friends to help you manifest these intentions (or even better realities) with elegance, ease and harm to none. Learn more about unseen friends at *LiveALifeYouLove. com/resources*.

Here's an example:

Dear Higher Self, Soul, & my other Unseen Friends,

Please help me with this creation.

I realize you can't do this for me, no matter how much you may want to. But help open my eyes to what stops me. Help me discover the beliefs that sabotage me. Inspire me to think of the most exciting actions to take. Open my eyes to the signs that will inevitably arrive. And help me stay in joy and feel deeply grateful for the gift of this life and all of the wonderful abundances that come my way. Thank you.

Love,

me

success!
Here's what happened

This is where you write about your dream manifesting in your reality. You'll note the date, and whether you recorded the success in your Success Journal. (Get yours at ***LiveALifeYouLove.com/product/success-journal***)

What you have created may not be the whole dream, and that's okay. You may want to start another dream section for the next level of your dream. However, be sure to celebrate whatever level or portion of the dream you did achieve, because it has landed in your reality, and you created it!

you are a

courageous being

to have made the choice to incarnate on this planet. Only those with strong will, love, and dedication to growth are brave nough to come here.

— Boni Lonnsburry

dream #1

....

....

....

....

dream #1 ....
....
....
....

looks like ....
....
....
....
....

feels like ....
....
....
....
....

I'll know I have it *when*

How having this dream *will change my life*

> *"It is not by knowing the theory that you create a wonderful reality. It is by doing the work."*

- Boni Lonnsburry

My *intentions* for this dream

techniques I completed

action steps I took

Beliefs I *changed*

signs I received

How I stayed
positive + expectant

....

....

....

....

....

....

my request for assistance

....

....

....

....

....

....

success!
Here's what happened

Date success was recorded on

notes

....

....

....

....

....

....

....

....

....

....

....

....

NOTE | **When you create successes (little or big), please let us know! Your success inspires others! Visit *LiveALifeYouLove.com/Inspire/#Simple2***

you deserve.

*Just because you are
alive, you deserve your every
dream coming true.*

-Boni Lonnsburry

dream #2

....
....
....
....

dream #2 ....
....
....
....
....

looks like ....
....
....
....
....

feels like ....
....
....
....
....

I'll know I have it *when*

....
....
....
....
....

How having this dream *will change my life*

....
....
....
....

"If you could let go of what you think things should look like, and instead focus on the essence of your desires, you would find yourself living in absolute bliss—without a care or a desire in the world."

- Boni Lonnsburry

My *intentions* for this dream

Techniques I completed

....

....

....

....

....

....

....

....

....

....

....

....

....

....

....

....

....

action steps I took

Beliefs I *changed*

signs I received

....

....

....

....

....

....

....

....

....

....

....

....

....

....

....

....

....

How I stayed *positive + expectant*

....

....

....

....

....

....

my request for assistance

....

....

....

....

....

....

success!
Here's what happened

....

....

....

....

....

....

....

....

....

....

....

....

....

....

Date success was recorded on

notes

··

··

··

··

··

··

··

··

··

··

··

··

NOTE

When you create successes (little or big), please let us know! Your success inspires others! Visit *LiveALifeYouLove.com/Inspire/#Simple2*

There is no moment
more powerful than
than now.

It creates your every tomorrow.

– Boni Lonnsburry

dream #3

....

....

....

....

dream #3 ....

....

....

....

looks like ....

....

....

....

....

feels like ....

....

....

....

....

I'll know I have it *when*

....
....
....
....
....

How having this dream
will change my life

....
....
....
....

*"There is beauty in the everyday. There is wonder in the mundane.
There is meaning in the tiniest details of your life. Begin to look at
your world with new eyes. Appreciate everything you create."*

- Boni Lonnsburry

My *intentions* for this dream

techniques I completed

action steps I took

....

....

....

....

....

....

....

....

....

....

....

....

....

....

....

....

....

....

Beliefs I *changed*

signs I received

How I stayed *positive + expectant*

....
....
....
....
....
....
....

my request for assistance

....
....
....
....
....
....
....

success!
Here's what happened

....

....

....

....

....

....

....

....

....

....

....

....

....

Date success was recorded on

notes

NOTE

When you create successes (little or big), please let us know! Your success inspires others! Visit *LiveALifeYouLove.com/Inspire/#Simple2*

Allow yourself to celebrate

what you are creating

before it manifests,

as it is manifesting, and after it has manifested.

— Boni Lonnsburry

dream #4

....

....

....

....

dream #4

....

....

....

....

looks like

....

....

....

....

feels like

....

....

....

....

....

I'll know I have it *when*

How having this dream *will change my life*

"Trust the universe and it's impeccable knowing and timing about how to deliver your dreams. What may seem like a dead-end to you may be the fastest way for the universe to make your dreams a reality."

- Boni Lonnsburry

My *intentions* for this dream

Techniques I completed ....

....

....

....

....

....

....

....

....

....

....

....

....

....

....

....

....

....

action steps I took

Beliefs I *changed*

signs I received

....

....

....

....

....

....

....

....

....

....

....

....

....

....

....

....

....

How I stayed *positive + expectant*

....

....

....

....

....

....

my request for assistance

....

....

....

....

....

....

success!
Here's what happened

....

....

....

....

....

....

....

....

....

....

....

....

....

....

Date success was recorded on

notes

....

....

....

....

....

....

....

....

....

....

....

....

NOTE | When you create successes (little or big), please let us know! Your success inspires others! Visit *LiveALifeYouLove.com/Inspire/#Simple2*

The more you get to know your dream—the more intimate you are with it—the more satisfaction you will have in creating it

and the quicker
it will manifest.

\- Boni Lonnsburry

dream #5

dream #5

....
....
....
....
....

looks like
....
....
....
....
....
....

feels like
....
....
....
....
....

I'll know I have it *when*

....

....

....

....

....

How having this dream
will change my life

....

....

....

....

"What would you do, if you knew you could not fail? Who would you be, if you were certain you would succeed? The only things between that reality and your current reality are your thoughts, feelings, and beliefs—change them."

- Boni Lonnsburry

My *intentions* for this dream

techniques I completed ....

....

....

....

....

....

....

....

....

....

....

....

....

....

....

....

....

....

action steps I took

Beliefs I *changed*

signs I received

How I stayed *positive + expectant*

....

....

....

....

....

....

my request for assistance

....

....

....

....

....

....

success!
Here's what happened

....

....

....

....

....

....

....

....

....

....

....

....

....

Date success was recorded on

notes

....

....

....

....

....

....

....

....

....

....

....

....

NOTE | When you create successes (little or big), please let us know! Your success inspires others! Visit *LiveALifeYouLove.com/Inspire/#Simple2*

Nothing you create "out there"
will truly bring you happiness.

happiness
is an inner choice.

– Boni Lonnsburry

dream #6

dream #6

....

....

....

....

looks like

....

....

....

....

....

feels like

....

....

....

....

....

I'll know I have it *when*

How having this dream
will change my life

*"The journey to become a masterful creator of your world is not a short one.
It is a life's calling. It is everyone's life calling. It isn't a new way of doing
your life. It is a new way of being, from moment to moment, in your life."*

- Boni Lonnsburry

My *intentions* for this dream

techniques I completed ....

action steps I took

....

....

....

....

....

....

....

....

....

....

....

....

....

....

....

....

....

....

Beliefs I *changed*

signs I received

How I stayed *positive + expectant*

....
....
....
....
....
....
....

my request for assistance

....
....
....
....
....
....
....

success!
Here's what happened

....

....

....

....

....

....

....

....

....

....

....

....

....

....

Date success was recorded on

notes

....

....

....

....

....

....

....

....

....

....

....

....

NOTE

When you create successes (little or big), please let us know! Your success inspires others! Visit *LiveALifeYouLove.com/Inspire/#Simple2*

If you are creating correctly,

you won't really care

if your dream

manifests or not

because you will already be feeling all the wonderful

feelings you will have when you get it.

- Boni Lonnsburry

dream #7

....

....

....

....

dream #7

looks like

feels like

I'll know I have it *when*

....

....

....

....

....

How having this dream
will change my life

....

....

....

....

....

"Fear may come up for you as you move towards your dream. And if it does, welcome it—it is there for a reason. What are you afraid will happen? That is a belief. Change it. And move back into feeling the excitement!"

- Boni Lonnsburry

My *intentions* for this dream

techniques I completed ....

....

....

....

....

....

....

....

....

....

....

....

....

....

....

....

....

....

....

....

action steps I took

Beliefs I *changed*

signs I received

How I stayed *positive + expectant*

....
....
....
....
....
....

my request for assistance

....
....
....
....
....
....

success!
Here's what happened

....

....

....

....

....

....

....

....

....

....

....

....

....

Date success was recorded on

notes

....

....

....

....

....

....

....

....

....

....

....

....

NOTE | When you create successes (little or big), please let us know! Your success inspires others! Visit *LiveALifeYouLove.com/Inspire/#Simple2*

gratitude
grows more reasons to feel grateful.

What are you grateful for?

— Boni Lonnsburry

dream #8

dream #8

looks like

feels like

I'll know I have it *when*

....

....

....

....

....

How having this dream *will change my life*

....

....

....

....

"It will take a while to retrain your brain. Initially negative thoughts and emotions will come up. When they do, simply say, 'Cancel, cancel.' And remember...positivity is vastly more powerful than negativity."

- Boni Lonnsburry

My *intentions* for this dream

techniques I completed

action steps I took

Beliefs I *changed*

signs I received

How I stayed *positive + expectant*

....

....

....

....

....

....

my request for assistance

....

....

....

....

....

....

success!
Here's what happened

Date success was recorded on

notes

....
....
....
....
....
....
....
....
....
....
....
....
....

NOTE | When you create successes (little or big), please let us know! Your success inspires others! Visit *LiveALifeYouLove.com/Inspire/#Simple2*

The essence you seek
is the essence you must put forth to
receive your dream.

– Boni Lonnsburry

dream #9

....

....

....

....

dream #9

looks like

feels like

I'll know I have it *when*

....
....
....
....
....
....

How having this dream
will change my life

....
....
....
....

"Dream new dreams and plan on a wondrous future, but also be here, now, in this present moment. It's a paradox—dreaming the future and being excited about it, while being firmly in the 'now' and loving every second of it."

- Boni Lonnsburry

My *intentions* for this dream

techniques I completed ....

....

....

....

....

....

....

....

....

....

....

....

....

....

....

....

....

....

action steps I took

Beliefs I *changed*

signs I received

....

....

....

....

....

....

....

....

....

....

....

....

....

....

....

....

....

....

How I stayed
positive + expectant

....
....
....
....
....
....
....

my request for assistance

....
....
....
....
....
....
....

success!
Here's what happened

_____

_____

_____

_____

_____

_____

_____

_____

_____

_____

_____

_____

_____

_____

Date success was recorded on

notes

....
....
....
....
....
....
....
....
....
....
....
....
....

NOTE

When you create successes (little or big), please let us know! Your success inspires others! Visit *LiveALifeYouLove.com/Inspire/#Simple2*

Keep your dreams close to your heart. Let them matter to you. Think of them as

wonderful
new friends,
whom you love and want to nurture.

- Boni Lonnsburry

dream #10

....

....

....

....

dream #10

looks like

feels like

I'll know I have it *when*

....

....

....

....

....

How having this dream
will change my life

....

....

....

....

"Everyone has the ability to create a life they love. Everyone. Some are not ready for this news yet. Some have more pressing issues to deal with, such as surviving day to day. But if you are reading this, you are ready."

- Boni Lonnsburry

My *intentions* for this dream

techniques I completed

action steps I took

Beliefs I *changed*

signs I received

How I stayed
positive + expectant

....

....

....

....

....

....

....

my request for assistance

....

....

....

....

....

....

success!
Here's what happened

Date success was recorded on

notes

....

....

....

....

....

....

....

....

....

....

....

....

....

....

NOTE

When you create successes (little or big), please let us know! Your success inspires others! Visit *LiveALifeYouLove.com/Inspire/#Simple2*

*There is nothing more you
could do, say, or be that would make*

you more worthy,

more divine,

*or more loved by God and Goddess
than you already are.*

- Boni Lonnsburry

dream #11

....

....

....

....

dream #11

looks like

feels like

I'll know I have it *when*

....

....

....

....

....

How having this dream *will change my life*

....

....

....

....

....

"The 'things' are the 'side effects' to living a life of joy, passion, love and unending imagination."

- Boni Lonnsburry

My *intentions* for this dream

techniques I completed ....

....

....

....

....

....

....

....

....

....

....

....

....

....

....

....

....

action steps I took

Beliefs I *changed*

signs I received

How I stayed
positive + expectant

....

....

....

....

....

....

my request for assistance

....

....

....

....

....

....

success!
Here's what happened

....

....

....

....

....

....

....

....

....

....

....

....

....

....

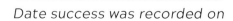

Date success was recorded on

notes

....
....
....
....
....
....
....
....
....
....
....
....

NOTE

When you create successes (little or big), please let us know! Your success inspires others! Visit *LiveALifeYouLove.com/Inspire/#Simple2*

no matter what happens

in your world, there is always a reason that it happened. If you don't like what happened, find the

reason & change it.

- Boni Lonnsburry

dream

#42

....

....

....

....

dream #12

looks like

feels like

I'll know I have it *when*

....

....

....

....

....

How having this dream
will change my life

....

....

....

....

....

"The real win is in finding the emotional space inside of you that feels so strongly that you already have the dream, that you no longer care if it manifests."

- Boni Lonnsburry

My *intentions* for this dream

techniques I completed ·····

···
···
···
···
···
···
···
···
···
···
···
···
···
···
···

action steps I took ....

....

....

....

....

....

....

....

....

....

....

....

....

....

....

....

....

Beliefs I *changed*

signs I received

How I stayed
positive + expectant

....

....

....

....

....

....

my request for assistance

....

....

....

....

....

....

success!
Here's what happened

Date success was recorded on

notes

....
....
....
....
....
....
....
....
....
....
....
....

NOTE | When you create successes (little or big), please let us know! Your success inspires others! Visit *LiveALifeYouLove.com/Inspire/#Simple2*

If you have cleared out all of the beliefs in opposition to your dream, there will be **no doubt** *in your mind about whether that dream will manifest. The only questions will be "When?" and "How will it show up?"*

— Boni Lonnsburry

dream #13

....

....

....

....

dream #13

looks like

feels like

I'll know I have it *when*

How having this dream
will change my life

"When I let go of control, I am amazed at how well things turn out. Not that it's always easy to do...believe me it isn't. But when I do manage it, my life works so much better than when I try to make things turn out a certain way."

- Boni Lonnsburry

My *intentions* for this dream

Techniques I completed

....

....

....

....

....

....

....

....

....

....

....

....

....

....

....

....

....

action steps I took

Beliefs I *changed*

signs I received

How I stayed *positive + expectant*

....

....

....

....

....

....

my request for assistance

....

....

....

....

....

....

success!
Here's what happened

....

....

....

....

....

....

....

....

....

....

....

....

....

....

Date success was recorded on

notes

....
....
....
....
....
....
....
....
....
....
....
....
....

NOTE

When you create successes (little or big), please let us know! Your success inspires others! Visit *LiveALifeYouLove.com/Inspire/#Simple2*

changing beliefs will
impact your reality
more than any other work you do. Set aside time
regularly to change beliefs.

- Boni Lonnsburry

dream #14

....

....

....

....

dream #14

looks like

feels like

I'll know I have it *when*

....

....

....

....

....

How having this dream
will change my life

....

....

....

....

....

*"You deserve to manifest all the abundance
you can imagine – and so much more."*

- Boni Lonnsburry

My *intentions* for this dream

Techniques I completed

action steps I took

Beliefs I *changed* ....

signs I received

How I stayed
positive + expectant

....

....

....

....

....

....

....

my request for assistance

....

....

....

....

....

....

success!
Here's what happened

Date success was recorded on

notes

....

....

....

....

....

....

....

....

....

....

....

....

....

NOTE

When you create successes (little or big), please let us know! Your success inspires others! Visit *LiveALifeYouLove.com/Inspire/#Simple2*

Every single person who has the success you seek is a sign that you can create it too.

– Boni Lonnsburry

dream #15

dream #15

looks like

feels like

I'll know I have it *when*

....

....

....

....

....

How having this dream *will change my life*

....

....

....

....

"When you feel gratitude, you are lifted to a higher resonance. It's quick. It's easy. You can do it anywhere. Make a list of all you are grateful for, and feel your resonance shift."

- Boni Lonnsburry

My *intentions* for this dream

techniques I completed

action steps I took

Beliefs I *changed*

signs I received

....

....

....

....

....

....

....

....

....

....

....

....

....

....

....

....

....

....

How I stayed *positive + expectant*

....

....

....

....

....

....

my request for assistance

....

....

....

....

....

....

success!
Here's what happened

Date success was recorded on

notes

....

....

....

....

....

....

....

....

....

....

....

....

....

NOTE

When you create successes (little or big), please let us know! Your success inspires others! Visit *LiveALifeYouLove.com/Inspire/#Simple2*

Also by
Boni Lonnsburry

The Map: To Our Responsive Universe,
Where Dreams Really Do Come True!

The Map Workbook

The Map to Abundance: The No-Exceptions Guide
to Creating Money, Success, & Bliss

The Map to Abundance Workbook

Messages from Your Unseen Friends: Volume I

Messages from Your Unseen Friends: Volume II

Life on Planet Earth: A User's Guide (e-book)

Gratitude Journal: A Magical Place to Multiply Your Blessings

Success Journal: A Magical Place to Record Your Triumphs

All of Boni's books are available at:
www.LiveALifeYouLove.com/Shop

About the
author

Boni Lonnsburry is the Chief Visionary Officer of Inner Art Inc., an expert on conscious creation, and the author of ten books, including The Map: To Our Responsive Universe, Where Dreams Really Do Come True! and The Map to Abundance: The No-Exceptions Guide to Creating Money. Success, & Bliss, which together have won fifteen awards, including the Nautilus Award and the Silver Benjamin Franklin Award.

By applying the Universal Law of Attraction, Boni transformed her life of poverty, loneliness, and despair to one of abundance, love, and joy. She now teaches others to do the same.

Learn more about Boni's work at
www.*LiveALifeYouLove*.com/ and *CreationSchool.com*

Made in the USA
Monee, IL
20 December 2022